WINDSOCKS
and
BOXES

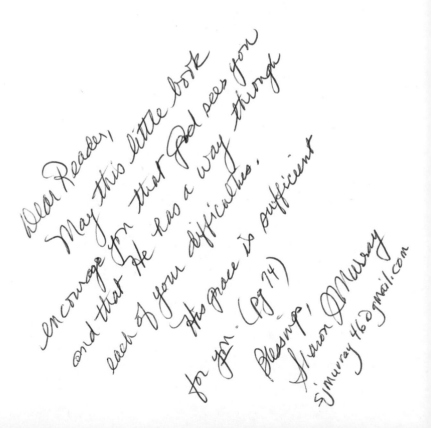

Dear Reader,

May this little book encourage you that God sees you and that He has a way through each of your difficulties. His grace is sufficient for you. (pg 74)

Blessings,
Sharon D Murray
sjmurray46@gmail.com

WINDSOCKS
and
BOXES

*Help for Living in a World
with Other People*

Sharon J. Murray

Print information available on the last page.

Rev. date: 08/31/2017

To order additional copies of this book, contact:
Xlibris
1-888-795-4274
www.Xlibris.com
Orders@Xlibris.com
756911

CONTENTS

To my father,
a kind man, who consistently saw the best in people
*The characteristic of the life of a saint is
essential elemental simplicity.*
Oswald Chambers

ACKNOWLEDGEMENTS

Thank you, Kimberly, for your early support – typing from my handwritten pages and from dictation, as well as finding cover ideas. You were great.

Thank you, Andrea, for teaching me some of the basics of Word documents and for the good laughs in the process.

Thank you, Lisa, Andrea, and Gretchen, for your wonderful editing skills that made this a better book page after page.

Thank you, Tim, for approving, and for making me happy.

All Oswald Chambers quotes are taken from *The Complete Works of Oswald Chambers,* © 2000 by the Oswald Chambers Publications Assn., Ltd. Used by permission of Discovery House Publishers, Grand Rapids, MI 49501. All rights reserved.

Hannah Hurnard quote taken from *Hinds Feet on High Places* by Hannah Hurnard. Copyright 1987. Used by permission of Tyndale House Publishers, Inc. All rights reserved.

CS Lewis quote from *That Hideous Strength* by CS Lewis © copyright CS Lewis Pte Ltd 1945. Used by permission

1

To Begin With

This book is not going to be everybody's cup of tea. Some people let upsetting words and actions roll off their backs or, at most, they fuss a bit and then get over it. But if you're like me and have to work hard to get over things, you are going to find some relief in these pages. You will see that God has an endless variety of ways to care for us.

The fact of the matter is, *everyone* has problems with *someone*, and if we are to maintain our sense of peace and well-being we need to have some tools for dealing with these problem people. I'm talking about our neighbors, our coworkers, and the people who impact our daily lives. I include people whom we love very much.

Now I tend to agree with Lucy of "Peanuts" fame when she declares, "I can't help thinking this would be a better world if everyone would listen to me." However, there are no two people in the world who are exactly alike, which means that no one I know agrees with me on everything. That leads to difficulties.

My husband is a teacher at a small Bible college. We live on campus along with the rest of the staff. I have lived in a close community for more than forty years. That leads to difficulties.

Supposedly there are people in the world who are open and up front about disagreements. I am not one of them. That leads to difficulties.

But I am interested in being at peace and I am interested in having an attitude that is acceptable to God. I believe that God is interested in those same ends. And that leads to some ways out of difficulties.

Of course, sometimes it is the appropriate thing, when something upsets you, to go and talk it out with the person who has offended you. There are books written on how to do that. This book is not one of those. This book is concerned chiefly with the times when, for one reason or another, talking it out is not an option. Or it can be used to help you get your spirit calmed *before* talking something through. Or it can be used when you *have* talked and it hasn't made any real change.

Through the years, having had many run-ins with other people's personalities or ideas or ways of doing things, I have collected a number of tools that I can pull out on those occasions when someone doesn't do things the way I think he should.

Now, before I go further, I will note that not everything I say in this book is completely accurate. Sometimes I have changed details significantly to protect people's identities and sometimes I've changed details slightly for the sake of the story. Don't worry, you'll still get the point all right.

One other disclaimer. This book is not geared toward people who have suffered serious abuse. I am not writing about dealing with evil people or evil deeds. I am writing about dealing with good people who do things that impact us negatively.

Also, you must realize that although I am recounting stories of difficulties with various people, these are people whom I have also appreciated. You know how it goes: one day someone causes you great distress, and the next day (well, maybe week) he does something that means so much to you, you forgive all. These stories, however, are about the days of distress.

The Bible promises us that God won't let us be tempted more than we can bear, but that He will with the temptation make a way of escape so that we can endure. These are some ways of escape that have helped me to endure in my everyday, real-life pains.

Your life will be different from mine, and your pains may be much greater than mine, but the principle stays the same: God has help for each of us "adapted to each time and place" and, we may add, "person."

If you have a problem person in your mind right now, I suggest you do not read this book all at once. When you come to a chapter that works for the situation, practice that suggestion and save other chapters for your next problem. If a simple pair of pliers will do the job, then use them and don't bother to keep rummaging through the rest of the tool box to see what else is there.

Or, better yet, treat this little book like a box of chocolates, and keep it handy for when you need a chocolate fix for your spirit.

2

The Way He Is

For every evil under the sun
There is a remedy or there is none.
If there be one, seek till you find it
If there be none, never mind it.
Mother Goose (1916)

Now, to introduce the first tool, let's go over some hypothetical situations, some of which you may recognize.

You've worked diligently on a project, done a fairly good job, and someone happens along and comments – in public – that it should have been done differently.

You've explained to your roommate how it really bothers you to have the dishes pile up. She remains oblivious: it doesn't bother her.

You realize that you didn't do something quite right, but an observer makes it sound as though you were seriously deficient. You want everyone to recognize that you weren't *that* bad.

One friend or another points out that you neglected something, that you've wasted your money, that you're too picky, that you aren't raising your children properly, that *your* problems don't amount to much.

The possible scenarios are endless. Your husband says...Your wife thinks...That person drives you crazy by...This one makes you feel...He never...She always...And you end up feeling irritated, hurt, or angry.

There are a number of tools that will help out in these instances, but the one I am suggesting here is The Three Simple Statements.

Try them. Say them over to yourself and see what relief it brings to simply state the facts.

1. That's the way he is.
2. That's the way he always has been.
3. That's the way he always will be.

These statements help me to reconcile myself with the way that person operates. That's the way he is. No matter how much I wish he were different or how much I think he *ought* to be different, I realize that he *isn't* different. And so I change my mental stance. Instead of wasting my energy fuming over how he is, I use it to figure out how I can deal with things as I find them.

Different outlooks and different modes of operation bring pressure and distress, it's true, but that's an inevitable part of this life. We have to allow the other person to think and act differently from the way we would. And it doesn't help to feel shocked that they could ever think or act that way. If we *expect* it, it will help us to accept it and work with it instead of suffering or being irritated all over again each time they offend.

There's another angle: sometimes, even after we have worked to forgive someone for an offense, maybe multiple times, the next time they do something to upset us, all those other things we have already forgiven seem to have a way of scampering back again. *But* if we can look at it with this new lens, "That's the way he *is*," then we're not so apt to remember all those other times, because we have come to the studied conclusion that this is his mode of operation. It's who he is. Of *course* he's done all those things. He will do one of them again tomorrow, or next week, or next month. We accept the facts as they are, not as we wish they were. And we accept him as he is. It is a step toward inner peace for us, and probably a step toward more peace for him too.

Temperaments

I live next to a marsh. When I see a small furry head making its way down the stream, I pause to watch: is it a beaver or an otter? I can tell by whether it swims in a straight line tending strictly to business, or seems to frolic as it goes along. "After all," the otter says, "might as well have some fun along the way." I've never actually seen a beaver look with disdain at the otter's frivolous waste of time and energy, but I'm sure he must.

A study of the four basic temperaments is a great help in accepting "the way he is," as well as in accepting ourselves. Then we find out that it's not just him, it's his temperament; there are other people in the world like him. His way of thinking and acting has actually been classified! As has ours.

Temperaments should not be used as an excuse for bad behavior, but knowledge of them does give some understanding as to how a person could ever "say such a thing" or "act that way."

There are many books about temperaments or personalities. The one I read and found helpful years ago was Tim Lahaye's *The Spirit Controlled Temperament*. He uses the four major divisions described by Hippocrates:

the fun-loving Sanguine, the moody Melancholic, the calm Phlegmatic, and the get-there Choleric.

Someone else has compared the different temperaments to animals. Besides the do-it-right beaver and the fun-loving otter that we have already met, there are the kind golden retriever, and the take-charge lion.

There are also more detailed books on the personalities. I recommend a little study on this topic if you're not familiar with it all. It's another tool for helping us to understand that neither he *nor* I have something wrong with us. We're just people.

Or you could say *both* he and I have something wrong with us. The evening after I began writing this chapter, my husband asked if I wanted to hear a story. He was reading Joseph C. Lincoln's *Cape Cod Short Stories*, published in 1907. This was the opening sentence:

"We've all got a crazy streak in us somewheres, I cal'late, only the streaks don't all break out in the same place, which is a mercy, when you come to think of it." He goes on, "Jim Jones fiddles with perpetual motion and Sam Smith develops a sure plan for busting Wall Street and getting rich sudden. I take summer boarders maybe, and you collect postage stamps. Oh, we're all loony, more or less, every one of us."

We might as well accept it.

4

Accepting Ourselves

I heard an insightful anecdote at a conference years ago. A man and his wife had disagreed about something and then retired for the night. Suddenly the wife sat up in bed and declared, "Logic isn't everything. And feelings aren't nothing," and then lay back down again.

Sometimes the reason we're upset by what someone says is because it makes us feel stupid. Sometimes we feel that way whether anyone says anything or not! And when we're feeling stupid instead of accepting ourselves, it's hard to be doing the job God has given us to do.

When I say "accepting ourselves," I don't mean we should excuse weakness of character. I mean we should accept the things we cannot change – our God-given personality, our talents or lack of talents, etc. – and be content to work within those limits.

Now there are at least four good reasons why we should accept ourselves:

1. We won't be so likely to be hurt by criticism.
2. We won't be so likely to find fault with others.
3. We won't be finding fault with God's handiwork (us).

4. We will be free to do the work God has for us to do.

It's not just for our own comfort that we should accept ourselves; it actually makes us better people.

Of course, we always want to be growing where we need to grow. It's good to be inspired to improve in any area of our life. I love going to funerals because I hear good things about people and I leave wanting to be a better person. But there's a difference between being inspired to be better and being discontent with, or limited by, the way God made me.

"I believe everyone but myself," a friend once told me. She just assumed other people were always right. As a result she failed to recognize that she had valid reasons for the way she felt.

We get further faster if we realize there is a reason why we feel or act the way we do. It may not be the best or smartest way to feel or act, it may not be the way someone else would do it, but it might just be the only way we can operate.

One thing that militates against our accepting ourselves is comparing ourselves with others. Not long ago I had to take over the job of organizing "The Blue Notebook," a 3-ring binder full of menus and recipes used by the volunteers who cook for the conventions held here on campus. Now my friend Diane, whom I was replacing, was extremely capable: organized, efficient, and very good with computers. The notebooks she created were works of art. Color-coded works of art.

I sat down to create the notebook for an upcoming convention. My courage dropped lower and lower as I went. There was absolutely no way I was going to produce any beauty at all. A few handwritten notes with instructions for each day was as good as it was going to get. And sometimes I can't even read my own handwriting. I was feeling pretty dumb.

Fortunately, during this process, my friend of the "I believe everyone but myself" outlook called with a problem. I set out to encourage her that she was okay just the way she was: she didn't have to do things the way other people did.

That phone call transformed my whole attitude. Once off the phone, I realized that I, too, didn't have to do my job the way someone else did it. I didn't have to have a beautiful notebook! As my sister-in-law Helen encouraged me once when I was facing some new responsibilities, "You don't have to be wonderful, just adequate." What a relief.

And the cooks that convention did just fine.

Comparing ourselves with others is an automatic and natural thing to do, but it is a harmful practice. It's harmful whether we compare ourselves favorably or unfavorably.

"Walk before Me," God told Abraham. It's not our concern to be worrying about what other people are doing or what they are thinking of us. The One we want to please is God. The One we want to be like is Jesus. There's no feeling of competition there. Becoming like Him is utterly hopeless without His grace, but working with Him toward that end makes for delightful teamwork.

God gives each of us some work to do, and when He gives it to us He doesn't unmake the way He created us. He enables us to do that work acceptably within the context of the way He made us. It's okay if we have to ask for help to do it. It's a good thing, often, to find we must depend both on others and on God. People are generally willing to help, and God gladly gives guidance and help and wisdom when we need it. He isn't limited by our limitations – and it is our hands and feet and mouths that He uses.

God made us all different. Nothing I can do will make me quite as smart or efficient or witty or wonderful in any number of ways as others I could name.

Nonetheless, I have something good to add to the world if I will.

So have you.

5

Windsocks

Windsocks are one of my favorite tools. Have you ever seen them at a small airport? Or adorning someone's porch? The wind blows right through them and out the other end.

Sometimes people say things they shouldn't. Have you ever noticed that? It might be critical or just thoughtless, it might be barbed, it might be humiliating, or it might be only ill-timed. It might be said under pressure. It might be said because of a total misunderstanding.

For whatever reason it was said, if you let it hit you – let it enter into your heart – you will be hurt. So instead of being hurt, pull out your handy-dandy imaginary windsock and let all those words blow right through and out the other end. All words that should never have been said are windsock-worthy.

We generally feel that if someone says something to us, we should take it in. But when we're dealing with words that should never have been said, we just don't need to do that.

Windsocks can also be used for words that are just plain annoying. If her constant pessimism tends to dampen your spirit, why be damp? Windsock it. Is he a wearisome one-subject kind of guy? Maybe you could listen to a quarter of his monologue and let the rest go on out your windsock.

Sometimes people just need to say something, but if you don't need to hear it, windsock it! Why should their words disturb your peace?

You might even try windsocks on your own emotions when appropriate. Felt a stab of jealousy? It's not worth it. Windsock it. And what about that annoying driver in the other car? You can't do anything about his driving anyway except get high blood pressure. Why not just windsock your natural reactions and let him drive?

As a kind of reverse use, I have allowed other people to windsock my advice! Particularly, as a mother full of good advice, I have to allow my adult children to windsock my great suggestions.

But don't let these secondary uses distract from the main purpose of the windsock, which is where its chief value lies: letting those upsetting words that should not have been said, or at least not said that way, go flying through and out the other end. Gone.

My daughter Andrea has taught this to her high school students. "People are stupid," she says. "They say stupid things. Windsock those words." Later, Bob makes a teasing remark to Pete that hits a little too close to home, and Andrea sees the fallen countenance. "Windsock it, Pete," she says, and Pete remembers. Sometimes she has to be more discreet and catch Pete's eye as she stands behind Bob and mimes, using one hand to gently waft the words into the imaginary windsock she holds at her side.

At times, it's after the fact, rather than at the moment, that I think to use my windsock. Even so, it works to

diffuse the upset feelings. People sometimes say, "Just let it go." Well, windsocks are a way to visualize doing just that.

Most of the time I can do this in my head, but once or twice – when out of sight of the person who has just said some especially-hard-to-take words – I have made my arms into a circle beside me to help me actually be able to let those words go. One time I saw my daughter Kimberly practically shoving some words into her windsock!

But the funniest story was one Andrea told me after a recent Super Bowl game. She and some friends were watching the game in the home of one of her students. They cheered like everything when their team made an unbelievable interception to save the game. But then, with twenty seconds left, someone threw a punch and a brawl broke out. Andrea and the others began screaming at the TV screen, "Don't get a penalty! Don't blow it now, guys!" Suddenly she became aware of her student's mother screaming, "Windsock it, guys! Windsock it!

6

The Throne

Now I come to the very best help of all. It has often been my first and last line of defense. It is described in the book of Hebrews, the fourth chapter, right at the end. "Let us therefore draw near with boldness unto the throne of grace, that we may receive mercy, and may find grace to help us in time of need."

The Throne is there for any and every weakness, fault, sin, or struggle we ever have, and that includes attitude adjustments.

This is the greatest place to run to when I'm really upset with someone. It is my desperation measure, and it works beautifully. Now when I'm talking about grace-to-help-in-time-of-need, I'm not talking about the grace that has saved us from our sins; I'm talking about what someone once described as "the touch of the divine in the human heart." I'm talking about real help when I need it. When I'm angry. When I'm resentful. I'm talking about getting what I need, from heaven, to be what I should be in my heart, my attitude, my spirit.

I get this help by running, boldly even, sure of my acceptance, to the throne of grace – right to God. I tell Him where I've been wrong in my attitude and ask for *mercy* for that sin, yes, but I go right on to ask for *grace* – help – change – *something* so I won't continue to have a wrong attitude toward one of His children. And that's the end of my responsibility. Whew. I have asked, and now it's over to Him to work it out. I have transferred the problem.

Let me give you an example. Years ago, before I had come to the firm conclusion that my choleric husband deeply and thoroughly loved me, I developed what I came to call my "Magic Prayer." I would get my feelings hurt by the way he'd say something and the hurt would very quickly turn to anger. Fortunately I have a phlegmatic temperament which means I don't react immediately on the outside. Instead, I go quiet. This would generally give me time enough, after my husband's misspoken words, to make it to my bedside without having given an angry retort.

I would get down on my knees, and first of all confess that I was wrong wherever God saw I was wrong. I knew I was wrong to some degree because of the anger I was feeling, but I wouldn't try to figure out just what percentage I was wrong, and what percentage I was justified in feeling as I did; I would simply bow to God's standard. Whatever God required of me under those circumstances I was in agreement with, even if I wasn't sure exactly what those requirements were. Next I would ask for mercy – forgiveness for my sin. And then I would ask Him for "grace-to-help-in-time-of-need." And I found, over and over again, that by the time I got up from my knees, my spirit had changed.

That was the magic. Of course, we know there was no real magic; I had done business with God. There was a transaction between us: He had something to give me, and I took it. And *then* I could go to my husband and simply say, "When you said... it made me feel...." And because my spirit had been softened, he could hear me in such a way as to be able to give a soft answer back and smooth things over. What a wonderful tool.

Now I will admit, the prayer hasn't seemed quite so magical when I have used it for people other than my husband, perhaps because I'm not so invested in those relationships. The answer doesn't always come as quickly or as thoroughly, but many many times I have made my request known at the throne, taken the grace-to-help-in-time-of-need by faith, and found a definite change in my attitude. If I need to come repeatedly, I do – and find repeated help. And in the meantime, I generally stay quite relaxed about it, knowing that the ball is now in God's court. God doesn't fail to keep His promises. He delivers.

7

He Was Wrong

If you don't want to go to all the work of The Three Simple Statements of Chapter Two, try this one statement: "He was wrong." I'm not talking here about moral wrong; I'm not referring to sin. I'm referring to thoughtlessness, lack of sensitivity, mistaken judgment, etc.

I learned this tactic years ago when I felt some people had made a decision against me when they could just as well have made the decision in my favor. It was a more-or-less minor issue, but one that would nonetheless affect me negatively for a long while to come. I felt a little hurt and I kept fretting, thinking, "They were wrong."

I was standing in front of my kitchen sink one day, still fretting, when down from the direction of Heaven seemed to come these words: "They *were* wrong."

Oh! They *were* wrong. Well, then. That was understandable. I had been wrong plenty of times. Immediately I was able to just accept the fact of their wrongdoing. The hurt feeling left and I was at peace.

And so I use this simple tool over and over.

"He was wrong."

And each time, two things happen. The first is an amazing relief of spirit. It's strange because of course I am already feeling he was wrong. But something about making a definite statement to myself, "He was wrong," gives clarity and peace. Judgment has been given and I have been vindicated! There is a big difference between complaining in my spirit, and simply acknowledging the truth that the person did indeed do the wrong thing.

The second thing I notice is that almost immediately another statement follows in my mind: "I've been wrong plenty of times." I don't want people to remember those times or to hold them against me, so I find it almost automatic to be able to forgive the other person his wrong. Being wrong is not a big deal. We all take our turn at it.

Now don't be discouraged from using this tool when I tell you another thought that often follows awhile later. After I have become all peaceful because I know he was wrong and therefore I am off the hook, I find that in that place of peace I can see and admit, "Well, he did have a point." But then, a little humility feels good at the end of the day.

Sometimes I say, "She was right or she was wrong." I don't need to figure out which because either way shouldn't be a problem, as we shall see in the following story.

Years ago as I was sitting waiting for our morning chapel service to begin, someone came in and whispered to me that I should have done a certain job differently. I was furious. "She only said that because she doesn't like me," I told myself. "She wouldn't have said that to anyone else."

As the service started, the pastor presented a serious prayer request from a mother for her wayward daughter. I knew I was in no condition to pray, fuming as I was about those whispered words. But as I sat there, the thought came to me, "If she was right, I can take it; and if she was wrong, that's between her and God," and I was able to just let it go.

Moments later as I prayed for the needy daughter, I felt the Holy Spirit praying through me in an unusually powerful way. It seemed to me as though that prayer was God's way of letting me know that that had been the proper way of dealing with that critical remark.

8

Insights from Oswald Chambers

We have seen what we are not, and what God wants us to be, but are we willing to have the vision "batter'd to shape and use" by God? The batterings always come in commonplace ways and through commonplace people.

[S]uffering wrongfully will always reveal the ruling disposition, because it takes us unawares.

When disagreeable things happen, do we manifest the essential sweetness of the Son of God or the essential irritation of ourselves apart from Him?

The reason we are going through the things we are is that God wants to know whether He can make us good bread with which to feed others. The stuff of our lives, not simply our talk, is to be the nutriment of those who know us.

9

"Jesus, Help"

It was evening. I was in the first service of an eight-day church convention. I wanted to grow spiritually of course, but I was hung up on something. I was feeling bitter toward a couple people. As the speaker talked on about good things, I daydreamed of standing up to ask for prayer. "And good luck," I would say as I ended the request. I knew how I felt, and how I felt was bitter. I couldn't see how God Himself could change me.

However, that very morning in our regular chapel service, the speaker had told a story. His family had been praying together when his young daughter asked if she could pray. She had never attempted it before. "Sure," he told her, and he went on to describe the scene to us. "Scrunching up her eyes and distilling all she had learned about prayer, she said, 'Jesus, help.'"

After the opening service was over, I made my way back to my bedroom. "Jesus, help," I prayed as I walked, and by the time I had made it to my bedside and my knees, I noticed that my bitter heart was beginning to soften.

Jesus is a real person, as real (as George MacDonald put it) as though He lived on earth just last year. He remembers that we are dust. He understands our struggles, having lived among people Himself. He is able to help those who are tempted (Hebrews 2:18). And He was able, this time, to change the bitterness in my heart to peace.

10

"I Will Help You"

I believe it's called "Bible dipping." You open your Bible at random to see what God has to say about your present problem. I don't recommend it as a regular practice, nor do I consider it always reliable. However, I certainly believe God uses it sometimes to bring us comfort or help.

I was staying in a neighborhood where our children had lots of playmates. They were having a grand time together. Then one day I ran into the mother of one of the playmates and she told me that she felt my daughter was being a bad influence on her daughter. What a shock: I had been feeling the same about her daughter! It was a humiliating blow, perhaps especially because there was another friend within hearing distance. I hardly knew how to respond. I said nothing about my feelings, but I built up a huge head of steam as I continued to my destination. By the time I got there and happened to glimpse her going by again, I was ready to scream at her. Just then, something I had gotten from the Lord that morning came to me, and by the skin of my teeth I was saved from saying something I would have sorely regretted.

Instead, I all but raced to my room and fell to my knees. There I poured it all out to God. Then I picked up my Bible and opened it. "Fear not," I read (in Isaiah 41), "*I will help you.*" Well, I had thought she was the one who needed the "help," but God knew better, and I was glad to get this assurance for myself.

Another "Bible-dipping" time that was especially sweet was once when our young family was about to get the rare treat of having an extended time alone together. We were taking a long trip to visit some friends in another state. An elderly friend found out about it, and wrote to ask if she could go along with us.

I could hardly believe that the Lord would ask this of me. I certainly was in no frame of mind either for company on the trip or for a crowded car. "Dear Father," I prayed, "You know how much I've been needing a break... "

After my despairing prayer, I thought I would open my Bible to see if God had something to say to me. What I opened to was Mark 6, where I found some others who were in need of a break:

> And he saith unto them, Come ye yourselves apart into a desert place, and rest awhile. For there were many coming and going, and they had no leisure so much as to eat. And they went away in the boat to a desert place apart. And the people saw them going, and many knew them, and they ran together there on foot from all the cities, and outwent them. And he came forth and saw a great multitude, and he had compassion on them, because they were as sheep not having a shepherd.

Well, what do you know? Who could understand my feelings better than He? Jesus "hath been in all points tempted like as we are."

We made the trip with an extra passenger, and I remember nothing at all about it, so I'm sure it worked out just fine – as things so often do once God has adjusted our attitude. Certainly this was one of those times when God used this technique to speak peace to a hurting heart.

11

The Way It Seemed to Her

She said something that I really didn't like at all. I have no memory of what it was, but I remember that I was bitter about it. Bitter enough to pray. And to pray again a few weeks later when I realized that I was still bitter. And again a few weeks and then a few months later.

The following summer I was writing a letter to someone about grace-to-help-in-time-of-need. Back came the memory of whatever those terrible words were, and with it the realization that the bitterness was still there. In fact I could picture something inside me, shaped like a carrot, starting at the base of my neck and going down: a "root of bitterness."

Well, I knew what to do. Back to the Throne of Grace I made my way once more.

It was a day or so later when out of Heaven dropped this jewel, down, down, plop, right into my heart:

"That's the way it seemed to her."

Oh! Well, of course, if that's the way it seemed to her, then that's exactly what she would have said! Now I could have told you that obviously that's the way it seemed to her, but somehow it was different when God said it. It made sense in a way I could accept. That little jewel went right to the root of bitterness and dissolved it. For days afterward I was aware of a lovely empty hole where it had been.

You never know, when you come to that Throne, what form the grace is going to take. But God has a plentiful supply of it, and there's enough for each need, tailored to fit.

That's the way it seemed to her. That's probably the way it seems to her still. And even though it's still true that, "I can't help thinking that this would be a better world if everyone would listen to me," I have no right to demand, even in my mind, that someone else see things the way I do.

12

Dear Me

Twice in my life when I was under intense pressure, I have written myself a letter. Those letters were great! I was hearing from someone who really understood me.

"Dear Sharon," she wrote, "I'm so sorry for what has happened to you." This woman knew the entire situation, she knew the history behind the upset, she knew how I was affected, she knew the struggle, and she also knew my desire to end up with the right attitude.

What good advice she gave! She seemed to know just the things that would be helpful, and she encouraged me to take the steps I knew I ought to take.

One of those letters was so good I saved part of it for years so I could refer back to it.

You never know what wisdom you will pull out when writing to someone you care about who is in difficult straits!

This tool won't naturally appeal to everyone, but I invite you to try it. You might be surprised how much comfort and real practical help it will give you.

13

Circles

He drew a circle that shut me out –
Heretic, rebel, a thing to flout.
But love and I had the wit to win:
We drew a circle that took him in!

I have long loved these lines by Edwin Markham. I generally apply them not to people who have shut me out on purpose, but to people whose actions have made me feel distant from them.

Love and I have the capacity to draw a circle large enough to include not only a person but what I perceive as her failings. When I draw the circle around the person, it includes all that comes with her. I can choose to do that.

Once I have drawn the circle I have found it helpful to use the phrase, "She's in," when I think of or see that person. It serves as a reminder not only of the position I've given her, but of the attitude I am therefore taking toward her. And, sweetly enough, isn't that what Jesus has forever done for us in the sight of God? "She's in," He says. And we are.

Now let me illustrate. For several years I oversaw the kitchen here at the Bible School. This was not because I was a cook, but because I was available. In other words, I was on shaky territory.

One day several of the students and staff were working together in the kitchen, when the student who was cooking dinner that day as part of our vocational program asked me how to do something. I told her what I knew, only to have a more experienced woman speak right up and say, "That's not how you do it," and go on to tell the student the proper way to proceed.

Now this was not the first time I had been annoyed by something this woman had said. In fact it seemed to be a regular occurrence. I couldn't comprehend how she couldn't figure out that the things she said bothered people. Anyway, I'd had enough.

"Let me do it *wrong*," I shouted back at her. "It's my job!"

Well, actually, I didn't really do that; I just thought that answer up later. I forget now how I made my way through that particular provocation, but not too many days later when, again, a number of us were in the kitchen, this same woman made a statement that changed my whole perspective.

"I love the idea of royalty," she stated dreamily, "the queen who always says the right thing. But all my life I've had trouble saying the wrong thing."

"What?" I thought. "You know that?!" And somehow finding out that she knew her own weakness transformed my former picture of her. Instead of seeing her as an entirely dark figure who repeatedly impacted me in a negative way, I saw her as a fine white figure with one dark area that I realized I would occasionally run into. I grew to love her, appreciate her, and even go to her for advice!

Love and I were able to draw a circle around her that included the very thing about her that threatened me, and I was forever the richer for it.

14

Boxes

A friend was telling me about a situation with her new college roommate. "I just *mentioned* the problem and she reacted like that," she said. "I'll never do *that* again."

As I was mulling it over later, I suddenly saw something that would help the budding relationship. I realized my friend had put her roommate's reaction in the wrong box. She had put it in the "I'm hurt" box, which had left a little wall between them. If she had put it in the "challenge" box instead, saying, "Hmmm, next time I'll try saying that differently," she would have come away with an open attitude in which the friendship could continue to grow.

I began considering the boxes in which we put people's comments, and the boxes we could choose instead. There is a wide variety of boxes available and we get to decide for ourselves where the comments end up.

Some boxes really shouldn't be used for storage at all. Some are OK for temporary storage but shouldn't be used for long-term storage. And of course some boxes are designed for good, safe storage.

Boxes like "I hate him," "She's an idiot," or "I can never let that go," are never good for storage. The use of those boxes will hurt relationships. Even "She doesn't like me" or "I'm no good" are not helpful boxes.

The "I'm angry" and the "That hurt me" boxes are legitimate for short-term storage, but nothing should stay in them any longer than we can help. Those boxes are toxic. So as soon as we realize something has landed in one of them, it's time to start looking for the proper long-term box into which to transfer it.

What we've already learned in this book will provide us with some good storage possibilities. We can take something out of the "I'm angry" box and dump it into the "Throne of Grace" box. Or we can put it into the "He's wrong" box, and from there find it simple to move it into the "I forgive him" box, which of course is designed for long-term storage.

If we're very angry or very hurt, we may need to divide our grievances among several boxes: "That's the way he is," "That's the way it seemed to him," and "God allowed it," for instance.

Once I started working on it, I discovered that there are endless possibilities for box choices that will work. Here are some I came up with:

She didn't mean to hurt me.
He doesn't understand how that would come across.
Maybe she was already upset about something else.
He just wasn't thinking.
She can't help it.
He actually thinks that's the right way.
Maybe she feels threatened.
It really doesn't matter.
She means well.
He's doing the best he can.
She's insecure.
I can let that go.

You may come up with 20 or 100 more.

Many of the boxes on this particular list could actually be grouped loosely into one big box of "Understanding." Sometimes understanding why a person may have done something is all you need in order to take care of the problem. Other times that box is good for temporary storage, but then things need to be moved on. You may not be totally peaceful until you've been able to utilize the "I accept him the way he is" box or another good long-term storage box that you discover is there for your use.

Over the period of weeks when I was especially considering these boxes, something unforeseen happened to me. Two or three times old wounds came to mind and I found that each one still hurt. But now I realized that I didn't have to leave those wounds in the places I had put them so long ago. Interestingly enough, for those particular hurts, I didn't even have to figure out what box to put them in. Somehow just realizing that they didn't have to stay where they were made them disintegrate, and I was left with a wonderful feeling of new lightness.

To end this chapter I'll share a story a friend told me about the best box of all. I had just shared this box idea with her, and the next day she had occasion to remember it. She was asking God, "What box can I put this into?" when she got this response, "I'm putting *you* into My 'I love you' box." Ahhh.

Thank God for His box of love where we can be at rest even while we are waiting for His answer to our current distress.

15

Tidbits

We all think we have justification for the way we feel...
until we find out the other person's perspective.

What you tell yourself about a person or a situation matters.
A lot. Because you tend to believe what you say. So you
might want to think twice.

Our sufficiency is from God. Don't look for it somewhere
else.

Sometimes we do the right thing and it is not, even cannot,
be appreciated. But it is still the right thing to do.

We think, "I would never do that," but of course if we were
that other person, we would.

Is what he said out of character? Then rethink your
interpretation of it. For instance, if he said something that
sounded mean but he's not a mean person, then look for a new
interpretation of his words or of the thinking behind his words.

When it is the appropriate thing to talk things out, tread carefully. The goal is neither to put the offender in his place, not to prove that you are right, but simply to bring a better understanding between you.

16

Imagine That

'Fess up that this has happened to you too. You just found out that someone who irritates you has once again done something irritating. You are feeling quite justified in your indignation. He really is such a pain. Suddenly, you find out that it wasn't the irritating person that did it after all. It was your good buddy. "Oh well, ahem, there really is nothing wrong with doing that. It's certainly understandable. In fact, it's rather funny. Haha."

Now isn't that interesting. We thought it was the action that irritated us, but now we have to admit to ourselves that the irritation had nothing to do with the action, and everything to do with the person. Hmmm. Maybe we're not as nice or as objective as we thought we were.

So... let's use our imagination to help us accept each other. I've tried it this way: when someone does something I don't like, I've stopped to think, "How would I feel if it were Jane instead of Joan that was doing that?" Even if I'm still bothered, at least I realize that my attitude would be different if it were Jane, and that gives me hope that somewhere there must be grace for even this situation.

Another point while we're on the subject of imagination. When someone's words hurt us it's easy to imagine that we know their motives when really we don't. We'd do ourselves more good by imagining that they said those words because they trusted us not to take them wrong, rather than assuming they said them just because they were mad. Maybe they needed to vent and thought we were a safe person. Maybe it truly didn't occur to them that those words would hurt us.

And even if they are mad, sometimes the anger is actually rooted in something other than us. You know the old line about the boss yelling at the man who then goes home and yells at his wife who then yells at the child who then kicks the dog. Well, that is real life. I've seen it.

We never know what someone else is contending with. We'd do ourselves and the people we're dealing with a favor if we imagined that they had a valid reason for doing or saying what they just did or said, and consequently cut them some slack.

17

God Allowed It

"Is God in Everything?" The chapter bearing that title in *The Christian's Secret of a Happy Life* by Hannah Whitall Smith is the best thing I've ever read on this subject. If you don't own the book, I would recommend getting it, if only to read that one chapter. She shows beautifully how nothing can reach us unless God has allowed it.

For some reason God allows people to be the way they are. He also allows them to impact our lives. But He is a good God and He loves us as His own children, so we know He is mindful of how they impact us. That doesn't mean He's going to explain it all to us, but it does mean He knows how to make negative things work together for good. For us. All things. Read it for yourself in the book of Romans (8:28).

That truth doesn't always mean short term comfort. We still hurt. But it does help us to find a resting place in Him.

One day I thought I would take time to point out to God how He needed to change some of His children who, in my mind, were not acting as His children should act, and who, incidentally, were affecting me negatively. I got down on my knees and told Him what they were doing.

"I know," He seemed to answer me. Well! So I told Him something else they did.

"I know," came again. Well, really! So I told Him yet another thing they were doing.

"I know," came a third time.

Clearly, God had a different take on things from what I did. Maybe He was planning to work on those problems some year in the future, but evidently it was not shaking Him at the present time the way it was shaking me. In fact, His attitude changed mine enough that, unpremeditated, I ended my prayer with, "And I forgive them."

Hmmm. Maybe that was what was most important to God at the moment. Those other people may have needed God's work in their lives, but I couldn't be waiting around until they got it before I let God work in mine.

One of Hannah Whitall Smith's analogies is that of the medicine bottle. Some people are hard to swallow! Okay, she didn't say it that way, but isn't it true? Her point was that though people may be our "medicine," it is our wise Parent who doles out the proper dosage. Sometimes I think of it in Peter Rabbit terms: "One tablespoon of _____ to be taken at bedtime." Sigh. But these doses of hard people in our lives will do us good if we will accept them as from God's hand.

My nephew Dave once gave a helpful object lesson along these lines. He filled a container with water, which represented God's will. Then he dropped in a toy army man to represent us. There we were utterly submerged in God's will, just where we wanted to be. Then Dave dropped in a fork. Ouch, it hit us, but it was there only because God's will had allowed it. He added a knife. Ouch again. God's will again. Next he added some salt to represent the bitter things of life.

In my mind I labeled the fork Mr. X., the knife Mrs. Y., and the salt Issue Z, (X, Y, and Z all being sources of pain to me at the time). It was helpful for me to see them there as plain as day, all in God's will. They had been allowed their positions in my life by God; therefore He could use them for good in my experience.

I wrote a poem that illustrates this reality. One day I got a phone call from my daughter Andrea, who was feeling distraught over having been sorely mistreated. After I got off the phone, a phrase from Hamlet came to mind. Since Andrea teaches Shakespeare I thought it would be meaningful to her, so I got to work to see what I could produce that would be of comfort to her. Here it is.

Transformation

An arrow of outrageous fortune
    Sped her way
    And struck.
Full hard it hit the mark.

She staggered,
    Fell,
  And thought to swoon.
But Patience whispered, "Wait."

Instead she took the arrow out
  And hid it in her cloak
Where love and faith
  Transform such wares
And make them useful tools.

The Master Craftsman
    Took the tool
And chiseled loveliness,

Then with delight
    Beheld His art
And said,
"This too is good."

18

On Hold

She had the feeling that somehow, in the very far-off places, perhaps in the far-off ages, there would be a meaning found to all sorrow and an answer too fair and wonderful to be as yet understood."
Hannah Hurnard

"A hundred years from now you won't even care," my mother would say to me when I was upset by something or other. I don't remember getting much comfort from that wisdom in my youth, but by this stage in life I do realize that if I just wait for time to pass, I won't feel so bad. So sometimes I just put my emotions on hold and wait it out. (I actually use it more when I'm humiliated about something I've done myself, rather than when I've been upset by someone else, but the theory is the same for both.)

My mother, of course, was onto something. And not just for short-term waiting it out but for the literal one hundred years. I'm sure that when we get to heaven, we won't be complaining.

About anything.
Or anyone.

We've all doubtless read or heard of someone who has had a near-death experience. I once listened to a lady on TV describing her experience. "I had such a sense of knowingness," she said. "Everything made sense."

We can borrow the sense of peace that we know is coming and apply it now to our being misunderstood or misjudged or mis-anything-elsed. As my friend Alison quotes, "Everything is going to be all right in the end. If it isn't all right, it isn't the end."

I think of a very dear friend of mine who has gone on to be with the Lord. She had such high ideals about serving God with her whole heart and soul and life. But it seemed to me that life dealt her an unfair hand. Unfair and sad. She struggled on and did some beautiful things, but through such hard circumstances that it still makes me sad to think about it. God does allow unfair and hard things. We do have to overcome pressures from without and from within. That has been the story of heroes from time immemorial.

And yet I am convinced that every bit of the slogging along and slugging it out and pushing through has been made up to my friend many times over.

As it will be for us.

19

Put it in a Book

The summer my daughter Gretchen worked at a nursing home, she had a patient who was testing the limits of her patience. We came up with a helpful strategy: put it in a book. If we were reading a book about this kind of patient, we would respond with some good chuckles or with tenderness and understanding, rather than getting high blood pressure.

Perspective makes all the difference. In all arenas.

Any good novel has a protagonist and an antagonist. There's always a hero and his adversary. There's conflict. There are things the hero has to overcome. And we love to read about these things.

But when difficulties or difficult people come our way, we wish they would just go away. Haven't we sometimes thought, "My life would be great if only it weren't for_____"?

Of course, once we are through a difficulty we love regaling people with the awful details, but in the midst of it all, while the outcome is still uncertain and we're not sure the good guy (us) is going to win this one, we don't like the story at all.

We forget that conflict, struggle, and adversity overcome are what make the story worth reading.

So the trick is to "put it in a book" while we're in middle of the struggle.

Can't you just see that irritating person, that demanding boss, that grumpy patient or child or client, or even the entire office or neighborhood in an interesting book?

Okay, there he/she/it is in a book. Now what will we, the hero, do?

It's all very neat in the books we read. Our heroine, wise and good, meeting various difficult people, is above the petty or unreasonable or designing or opinionated party. She knows that "that's the way he is," and she works around it. She is bigger than it all. She might display a helpful sense of humor, but she at least has a healthy sense of proportion. She might sputter a bit, but she realizes that the other person's behavior does not have to dictate her response to it.

We rejoice when our hero makes the right choice and wins out. He is a man of integrity and would do the right thing even if it were to work to his detriment, even if no one were looking or would ever know.

What about us? Do we make right choices in the hard circumstances that other people cause?

Putting people in a book helps our perspective and helps us to see the possibility of being a hero, of doing what we ought to do or being what we ought to be, no matter the circumstances.

20

Tidbits II

Let people be wrong.

We don't get to choose our cross; it comes our way without our say. But it is still the one we are supposed to take up and carry.

Sometimes it's not that the other person needs to change, it's that our outlook needs an adjustment.

My pride, my allergic reaction to criticism, my need for "affirmation only, thank you," I finally identified as an idol. And the song says,

> "The dearest idol I have known, / Whate'er that idol be,"
> I said, "I'll tear it from Thy throne, / And worship only Thee."
> My soul was thus made free.

Amen.

As my grandfather's pastor put it, "Don't let some little miserable thing sour the whole day when a little wit from God and good humor on your part can make a merry time out of it."

I have discovered a life truth which I have experienced repeatedly in notable ways. It is this: When people don't take care of me, God does.

21

Love...Taketh not Account

My friend Bev told me this story. It helped me. It might help you.

When she became very critical over what a neighbor was doing, her husband was puzzled. "Why does what she is doing upset you so much when your dear friend is doing the same thing and you don't seem to mind at all?" he asked.

"Because I *love* my friend," she replied, and immediately heard what her mouth had said.

Abashed, she took the proper action: she took the problem to God.

And she didn't even pray for her neighbor to change her actions; she prayed that God would give her His own love for her.

And He did.

"In spades," she told me.

Bev described this as a watershed experience in her life, showing her God's power to change hearts and feelings from the inside. And to convey the lifetime change that God so graciously made, whenever she tells the story she adds, "I've loved her with tenderness ever since that time."

22

Just Because She Says It

Once upon a time, there was a student at our school who could rattle me. I don't remember now any of the specific things she said that made me feel threatened, but I do remember the mental rebuttal I came up with to help my own spirit:

"Just because she says it doesn't mean it's true."

Whew.

Some people are so forceful that you can be thrown by things they say even if you aren't wrong at all. They may have definite ideas about the way things should be run in the office, in the world, or in your life. They may be utterly convinced of the validity of their way of thinking about any given situation. Be discerning. Neither your actions nor your opinions need necessarily be governed by their convictions.

And just because she says it *strongly* still doesn't mean it's true.

23

A Word about Forgiveness

I had already heard that faith is a choice that is not dependent on feelings. And I had heard that love is a choice, also not dependent on feelings. But one day our pastor was talking about forgiveness, and I learned that forgiveness too is a choice. We choose to forgive. We say, "I forgive him."

Our pastor told about being mistreated by a superior in the military. He responded by making a choice: he forgave him. Interestingly enough, he didn't feel any different afterward, but whenever those hurt feelings came up, he would remind himself that he had forgiven the man. It took months, but eventually God backed him up with the desired feelings.

It is much like marking a voting ballot. When we vote it doesn't matter what we feel; the vote gets counted as we marked it.

So with our forgiving. We may still be upset by what someone has done, but we can choose to forgive him anyway.

When we don't forgive, we find ourselves imprisoned by our bitter feelings. And that is a very unhappy prison in which to be. Thank the Lord there is a way of escape, and it is called choice. As my son Dan once described it, it's as though there is no door on the prison, just an opening. We can walk out whenever we decide to. We can walk free.

24

It's Not Me

Before I got married, my mother shared a helpful story from my parent's younger years. She said that whenever she and my father would sit down to figure out the money, my father would end up hollering.

Suddenly, one day, it came to her: "It's not *me* he's hollering at; it's because the *money* isn't coming out right!" It was such a transforming moment that she passed it on to me – the one piece of everyday-type marriage advice that I can remember her giving me.

Then came the day in our early years of marriage when it came back to me. Tim came into the room, I said something, and he answered sharply. I remembered.

"Did something just upset you?" I asked.

"Yes!" he burst out, and went on to explain. Sure enough, it wasn't about me, it was about something else. Thanks, Mom.

Sometimes I've told myself, "That's his frustration talking." It pays to stop and think before we take something personally, because it may not be about us so much as it is about the fact that he just bumped his head, or he just missed that last turn he was supposed to take, or else something entirely unrelated just went wrong.

25

Hiding

We have a Hiding Place.

I use it often when I'm tempted to feel overwhelmed. I particularly use it in the middle of the night when problems seem to have a way of being bigger than usual.

But I have also used it when someone else has gotten angry at me for the way I've done something. Having someone angry at you is an unsettling experience. Time for a hiding place. Of course we need to do whatever we can to make things right, but we need to do that from a safe place emotionally. Someplace where we are totally understood, totally loved, and totally accepted.

That would be in God.

The Bible is full of references to this wonderful place. David the Psalmist repeatedly conveys a picture of the security there is in God. "Thou art my hiding place," he declares, and "God is a refuge for us."

David didn't try to tough it out alone. He was smart enough to look for his security not in his wits or in his troops but in his God.

His son Solomon understands as well: "The name of the Lord is a strong tower," he observes, "the righteous runneth into it and is safe." (KJV)

Isaiah agrees: "For Thou hast been... a refuge from the storm."

And then there are the comforting wings. "I will take refuge," says David again, "in the covert of Thy wings." And, "Hide me under the shadow of Thy wings."

Jesus Himself uses the picture. When He wept over Jerusalem, He said, "How often would I have gathered thy children together, even as a hen gathereth her chickens under her wings and ye would not!" (In the margin of my Bible, I wrote, "I would.")

Psalm 91 is perhaps the quintessential picture of the absolute safety "under the shadow of the Almighty." It includes, "He will cover thee with His pinions, And under His wings shalt thou take refuge."

Even Boaz spoke to Ruth of "the God of Israel under whose wings thou art come to take refuge."

Yes, along with all the other wonderful things God has done for us, He has provided a place where we can hide. He provided it because He knew we would need it. Actually, it's more than just a hiding place; it's a place for us to live. Away from other people. Away from problems. Away – in a sense – from ourselves.

Moses put it, "Lord, Thou hast been *our dwelling place* in all generations."

Jesus put it, "Abide in Me, and I in you."

> At the heart of the cyclone
> tearing the sky
> And flinging the clouds
> and the towers by
> Is a place of central calm;

So here in the roar of mortal things,
   I have a place where my spirit sings,
In the hollow of God's palm.
               Edwin Markham

Graciousness

My heart was moved by something my friend Linda told me.

She said, "I've learned to be more gracious as I've gotten older. Everyone has a reason for saying what they say." And this from someone who in her youth was already one of the most gracious and kind people I knew.

How we appreciate it when someone deals graciously with our words.

My Bible school roommate Lori was that way. In appreciation for how she treated my words, I once gave her this quote from Dinah Mulock Craik:

> Oh, the comfort – the inexpressible comfort of feeling *safe* with a person – having neither to weigh thoughts nor measure words, but pouring them all right out, just as they are, chaff and grain together; certain that a faithful hand will take and sift them, keep what is worth keeping, and then with the breath of kindness blow the rest away.

Wouldn't it be nice if we could always be that gracious with the words we hear?

Desperation

Unspeakable sorrow had come Job's way, and at last out of the depths of his anguish he spoke, bewailing the day of his birth.

One of his friends made an attempt to correct Job's attitude.

In defending himself, Job made a very instructive observation: "Do ye think to reprove words, seeing that the speeches of one who is desperate are as wind?" (Job 6:26)

The words of a desperate man are as wind. I have had a good number of occasions to remember that and make allowance for the words I am hearing. They are words which can properly be passed over, ignored. Except to be used as an indication of the depth of pain.

This might even apply to our children sometimes. "You never let me do anything," my young daughter, Kimberly, once said to me. Of course that was not the truth but it was an indication of how very much she wanted to do what I had just denied. It called not for defensiveness, but for a thoughtful explanation of why I had said no.

This type of "wind" is another place where we can use our windsock, this time out of kindness and understanding. We don't argue, try to convince, or respond in kind, but instead, allow the words themselves to pass by and just minister to the heart need.

My brother Lloyd was good at this. I remember one time when he had listened to a friend of mine who was going through profound suffering say some bad things about God. Lloyd didn't reproach her or correct her. He said to me simply, "We need to pray for her."

It's important not to take all words at face value.

28

Gifts

We had been married for more than 25 years the day I said something that deeply hurt my husband. His response deeply hurt me. We immediately took steps to rectify the situation, but I felt that our marriage would never be the same.

We went on living normally and being "fine," but still there was a scar. I don't know if Tim felt it or not. Likely he didn't, because that's the way he is – he gets bothered by something and then gets over it and forgets it. But I was hurting, not because of whatever he said (which I no longer remember) but because of the rift itself. Probably all the more because I had caused it.

Not too long after that our son Dan had a service at church in which he talked about the fact that God wants to give us good gifts. That was well and good for him – he had just gotten together with the gem of a girl who would become his wife. I, on the other hand, had just blown it when it came to being a good wife.

However, for an object lesson, he had borrowed from our home a gift-wrapped box which sat on the pulpit as he spoke. After the service, the box came home again.

Well, I decided to put the sermon to the test. I put the box on my dresser as a reminder and began to pray for God to heal that hurt. Some gifts come in small boxes, some in big, and I told God I was asking for a big one. I prayed – at least now and then – for weeks, perhaps a couple months. And as I prayed I could picture that big gift box beside His throne.

And then one day, all of a sudden, I realized that the healing had come. The hurt was gone. It was as though it had never happened.

That was a relatively big gift for me. But sometimes I think to ask for small things, too, like when I pray concerning one person or another, "Father, I ask you to take away the constraint between us," and down comes a little gift.

Dan was right. God loves to give good gifts to His children.

I'm certain that we carry stresses and strains that we don't need to, simply because it doesn't occur to us that God could actually change this little (or big) thing between us and another person.

Jesus once said to some people, "…ye will not come to me that ye may have life." Let's not make that mistake.

What gift do you need Him to give you?

29

Hmmm…

As I was about to enter the room, I heard the two ladies there discussing something concerning me. I turned and very quickly escaped back to my apartment. Whew! I definitely didn't want to hear all that.

At times, however, I haven't been able to escape. Sometimes, someone, for some reason, has thought it would be helpful to let me know what someone else has said about me. Now of course, second-hand compliments I'm quite delighted to hear. But when it comes to second-hand criticism, that's a different story.

Ever find out that you've been the topic of discussion when you weren't there to defend or explain yourself? Ouch. I have often said in my head, "You can think anything you want to about me, but please don't talk to someone else about it." After all, there's always the hope that the other person might not have noticed that failing yet!

Besides, we never like to feel like we're on the outside. If two people discuss me, they have become "the inner circle" and I'm the rejected one. Ouch again.

Well, I'll never get over minding being talked about, but I do sometimes think of this obscure verse from Ecclesiastes:

> Also, take not heed unto all words that are spoken, lest thou hear thy servant curse thee; for oftentimes also, thine own heart knoweth that thou thyself hast cursed others.

Maybe we haven't actually cursed another person, but haven't we crossed the line of kindness in the way we've complained about them to someone else? Or passed on a negative observation?

What do we learn from all this? Well, we learn that people will talk about us – sigh – but I think we should also learn not to take it so hard when we find that they have. "Take not heed."

And for ourselves, there's the "Do unto others" concept. How my father drummed into his eight children's heads, and practiced beautifully himself throughout a long lifetime:

If you can't say something nice don't say anything at all.

I sometimes think of this passage about King Nebuchadnezzar: "Whom he would he kept alive and whom he would he slew." He decided. He decided who would live and who would die. We can do that with our words. We can decide whose reputation lives and whose reputation dies, or at least is tarnished.

Anyone can be made to look just a little bit bad if we

try. It's easy.

Anyone can be put in a positive light if we try. That's sometimes a little harder but it can be done with a little effort.

It comes like breathing if we really love someone…

30

Tidbits III

"When I try, I fail. When I trust, He succeeds." – Corrie ten Boom

Don't love and appreciate your neighbor? The Bible speaks of "The precious sons of Zion, comparable to fine gold," and goes on to say, "How they are esteemed as earthen pitchers." It's possible that God may be seeing gold where we see earth. Everyone has something valuable to add to our life if we can only see it.

Sometimes we can look back and see what a pain we must have been to someone else. What were we thinking of!? Maybe we need to give other people room to be human beings too.

We think we have it hard sometimes, but so do the people we're dealing with. As Ishmael in *Moby Dick* says, "… the universal thump is passed around." His advice is, "and all hands should rub each other's shoulder blades and be content."

What an example we have in Joseph. After the appalling way his brothers treated him, he said, "Fear not… ye meant evil against me; but God meant it for good… I will nourish you, and your little ones." And then, "he comforted them, and spake kindly unto them" (Genesis 50:19- 21).

"Our job is not to see through one another, but to see one another through." (Author unknown)

31

One-Cent Molehills

A friend shared with us the Lesson of the Penny.

If you see a penny lying on the ground, it doesn't take up much of your vision. Even if you pick it up and hold it at arm's length, you see it, but you also see the grass, the trees, the sky, the people around you.

If, however, you decide to focus on the penny, and draw it toward one eye, closing the other eye, soon it obstructs the view.

That nearly worthless little piece of copper can obscure the beautiful world around you. Because you choose to let it.

Some of the hurts or irritations that come our way are not worth more than a passing acknowledgment. They happen, they hurt, but they aren't crucial. They're just a part of life.

Blessed is the man who can keep molehills as molehills.

Some people are even good at making molehills out of mountains. How we love those people in our lives. I remember a time in our earlier years of marriage when I upset Tim badly and then he upset me. When I went to go talk it out in hopes of making things better, he merely said, "It was just a bump in the road. No one said there wouldn't be bumps." I was amazed. I thought, "You call that a *bump* in the road!?" I had thought it was a mountain in the road, but I was delighted with his assessment of the event and was very relieved to just let it go.

But back to the one-cent molehills. Though we are speaking of small hurts, this is not necessarily a small thing. There are times when overlooking a wrong, compensating for someone else's shortcoming, or forgiving even a small hurt takes discipline and character. Sometimes it might even be called heroic. Small heroics, perhaps, and we might not think of ourselves as heroes when we refuse to take offense, but we certainly can make a difference by that kind of attitude.

I think of a missionary friend who had addressed the issue of her roommate's habit of letting the dirty dishes pile up, only to find that there was little or no change. She consequently decided that sometimes it was better to wash her roommate's dishes rather than have a bad attitude.

Doubtless there are heroics happening every day along these lines, and wherever that's so, the world is a happier place.

32

From Argh to OK

I have lived for seventy years, and I have come to the conclusion that God is not planning to change the people around me so that they will do what I think they should. Apparently it doesn't bother Him that they don't see things as I see them.

God lets people be people. Not only that, He is perfectly able to use them in spite of what I see as their flaws. He knows the plans He has for them and He knows how to get them where they need to be. He's working on it. It's even possible that they are already where He needs them to be for the time being. And though He's still working on me, it's just possible that I, too, am where I should be for the moment. God's work in our lives is an on-going process.

But He can use us where we are. Both of us. Together. And He has available to each of us, for the asking, all the help we need to survive each other's way of thinking.

Furthermore, my first choices are not always His first choices.

I want life to be easy; He wants me to develop character.

I would like to be good automatically; He knows I need to be dependent on Him.

I want people to like me; He chooses to have people mold me.

In short, He is God and I am not. He has a different perspective from mine and He has everything under control. And it's OK. He's got it.

33

Something Deeper

I had been struggling with a deep disappointment. I had lost some valued companionship. I didn't like the loneliness.

And then I read this sentence in *That Hideous Strength* by C.S. Lewis:

> "She seemed to him…
> to have in herself
>   deep wells
> and knee-deep meadows
>   of happiness,
> rivers of freshness,
> enchanted gardens of
> leisure…"

It struck me as a picture of someone who had her roots down deep in Jesus Himself. Jesus alone.

Oh, yes. Where I'd like mine to be.

34

More Grace

A few weeks before my mother died of cancer, she felt that God gave her this assurance: "My grace is sufficient for <u>you</u>."

"The *you* was underlined," she told me. What a comfort that was to her.

I believe the same is true for every one of us who wants it.

These chapters tell of places where God's grace has been sufficient for *me*. You may find in them nothing that works for you.

You don't have to.

God's grace is still sufficient for *you*.

And anyway, I will guarantee that no matter how many tools you collect, there will be times when nothing works, and you will just have to struggle your way through until God brings the answer that works for that particular problem at that particular time. Don't discredit the process. It's valuable. And it's always okay to be reminded that we need Jesus.

You will doubtless need to battle, but even as you fight your way through, know that God is not stumped. He is the

God of the impossible. He is fully aware of the situation. He knows you and what will work for you.

God is bigger than your biggest difficulties, bigger than the most challenging people with whom you have to interact, bigger than you. He is endlessly creative. And always faithful.

Make your way back to the Throne of Grace as often as you need to until you find the grace that helps *you* in the time of your need.

Be persistent. Be patient. God is *for* you and He will come through.